Too F🐾cking Cute *Animals*

A COLLECTION OF UNNECESSARILY ADORABLE ANIMALS

OLIVE MICHAELS

 sourcebooks

Copyright © 2022 by Sourcebooks
Cover and internal design © 2022 by Sourcebooks
Cover and internal images © Shutterstock, Getty Images, Freepik

Sourcebooks and the colophon are registered trademarks of Sourcebooks.

All rights reserved. No part of this book may be reproduced in any form
or by any electronic or mechanical means including information storage
and retrieval systems— except in the case of brief quotations embodied in
critical articles or reviews— without permission in writing from its publisher,
Sourcebooks.

Published by Sourcebooks
P.O. Box 4410, Naperville, Illinois 60567-4410
(630) 961-3900
sourcebooks.com

Printed and bound in China.
LEO 10 9 8 7 6 5 4 3 2 1

Introduction

Ah, animals. Particularly the unbearably adorable and excruciatingly cute. Don't you ever want to tell them to fucking take it down a notch?

This book is for people who love animals but occasionally need them to calm the hell down with how cute they can be. Sure, you could coo over the little cuties, but sometimes they just need to be told to stop being so damn precious! It's overwhelming! Here you'll find dogs playing dress-up, cats with no business fitting inside teacups, and wildlife being so damn delightful that it's downright un-fucking-fair. So get ready to swear out that serotonin and show your affection in the most profane way possible. Catharsis, here you come!

Yeah, I'd be **fucking surprised** if I were
the **cutest monkey** in existence too.

YOU CUTE ASSHOLES.

**Stay still long enough
for me to scoop you up and**

GTFO!

I make the **same face** when I see **YOU,** you **adorable motherfucker.**

What are you two cuties laughing about? All the ways you're cute as hell?

I don't know whether to be **delighted** or **threatened** by this outrageously cute motherfucker.

This is why reindeer fly instead of fucking run!

Can the brain **overload** from seeing too many **cute-ass** puppies?!

Am I dreaming?
Or is there a super fucking cute ferret **ASLEEP** in my sweater?

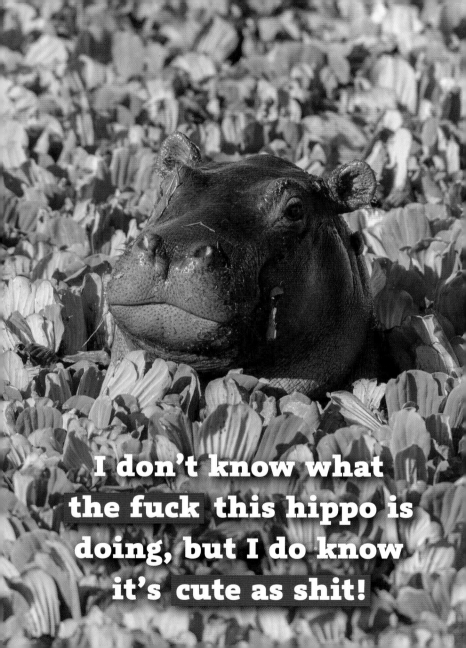

I don't know what the fuck this hippo is doing, but I do know it's cute as shit!

Well shit,
I could stare
into your
lovely eyes
all day!

The only thing *devilish* **about you is how devilishly cute you fucking are.**

The saying is "stop and smell the roses," but you're so cute I'll let this shit slide.

This pup's crooked grin is fucking everything.

These cute little fucks really just go about their days smiling, huh?

Is this an invitation to scoop
you up and **hug the shit** out of you?
Because if it is— **I'M IN!**

Not one but *two* baby elephants playing with their mom?
Shut the hell up!

I **WAS** going to brush my teeth...

...but I **GUESS** I've got to look at this cute fuck instead!

This adorable dog may be **sick** of this **cute shit,** but I'm sure as fuck not!

For fuck's sake, this duck is acting like he's a superhero!

ALL RIGHT, WHO SNUCK A TOY INTO THIS BOOK ABOUT ANIMALS? THE CUTENESS IS UN-FUCKING-REAL.

Don't you get tired of looking so fucking cute all the time?

Welcome to the world! Thank you for being cute as fuck!

Fuck, I bet this sweet bunny's fur is **even softer** than the **rose petals!**

Apparently the cutest fucking snuggles are on the savanna.

Hey! Someone lost their cute-ass teddy bears!

What a playful little shit, **sticking his tongue out at** me!

What the hell?!
Alpacas *and* llamas
are both fucking
precious?!

Pretty sure an **animated princess** is looking for your **cute ass!**

I don't know what
he's running from,
but you bet your ass
I'll run too!

Clearly these two are **best fucking friends.**

This guinea pig has mad-scientist hair, and I'm fucking living for it.

No matter **how** angry you get, you're still **so damn** adorable!

How **dare** you fucking taunt me with the softest, most adorable hug I've ever seen?

This cute
motherfucker is
getting ready to
audition for a heavy
metal band. He takes
it very seriously, as
you can see.

I wish I looked that damn cute when I'm tired AF.

Hedgehog + mushroom = cutest shit ever.

The cozy-ass sweater.
The leaf hat.
The adorable fatness.
Where do I
fucking start?

Clearly someone fucked up, why are there three damn clouds here?

I would do **fucking anything** to hang out with this **cute-as-hell** sloth.

If these two mice are out here living their best lives, then we sure as fuck can too!

Real fucking friendship is when your buddy licks your ears for you.

No one **likes** PDA...
unless it's these
cute-ass marmots
doing it!

Look at these matching motherfuckers!

Fuck

Swan Lake,

this shit is

WAY cuter!

Evidence suggests that these are in fact the same cute-as-shit animal. Looks at those ears!

F
for camouflage,
A+
for fucking cuteness!!

Yes, you can have a hug, you adorable motherfucker!

Whatever this little hermit crab wants, this little hermit crab **fucking gets.**

That's it, baby squirrels are fucking illegal —they're too cute!

How *dare you* look that tiny and adorable and be giving me that *sweet fucking look*.

Fuck these lambs and **fuck** that picturesque field!

Must.
Fight.
Urge.
To.
PET.
Adorable.
SPIKY.
Asshole.

You put those cute-ass paws
down right now!

Y'all look like snuggling mangos and it's fucking *unfair.*

Get THE FUCK out of his way, he's got BUSINESS to attend to!

Work those fucking angles, you adorable little seal!

The **cutest** damn **lunch break** ever!

How did the photographer not fucking die of cuteness?

Put this **poolside pug** in a **music video** right the **fuck now!**

Blissed out like a basic bitch.

The only thing fucking cuter than one fox **is** two foxes!

WELL DAMN, I didn't know dog hugs were a thing. Have I been befriending dogs wrong?

I'm putting my foot down!
It's impossible for a real animal
to be **THIS** fucking adorable!

Is this even real life anymore? This shit is straight out of a greeting card.

Fuck your wrinkles, you precious pup!

Baby alligators giving each other hugs makes me happy as hell.

I can bear-ly resist joining in on this cute-as-hell dance!

Between the flowers, the sunshine, and the adorable fucking nose, my heart might not survive.

This duckling
is ready to take on
the *fucking world*
and I am here for it.

Your winter fashion is un-fucking-matched!

Quit hogging all the blankets, you adorable asshole!

**Sweet dreams
to you and your
cute-as-hell stripes!**

I feel like they're plotting something...

You can't tell me they're not about to drop the most adorable damn album of the year.

This sleepy fawn is going to make me fucking explode from cuteness!

Psst. *Psst. Are you awake?
Just wanted to say you're cute as fuck.

How **the hell** did I stumble into a damn shampoo commercial?

This cute motherfucker can laugh at me as much as he wants!

Never thought a stingray would melt my heart, but here we fucking are!

Mama bear is
dealing with a
triple fucking threat!

Where **the hell** is your other ear, you **adorkable motherfucker?!**

Look at these cute-ass ham-stars!

See, being lazy is fucking adorable!

Commuting in the rain is the fucking worst, but at least this little guy still looks cute as hell!

This cute fluff is living the best damn life and I am crying.

Too.
Fucking.
Fly.

This cute-ass koala-ty time
is too. Fucking. Much.

I'm pretty damn sure that's not where you belong...but you're so precious, you can stay!

Fuck the fuck off with that tiny little face!!

They're clearly in the middle of a cute-ass game

of duck, duck, chick!

Cover your mouth when you sneeze!
What are you, a fucking animal?

Oh fuck right off, you expect me to believe you're **naturally** this cute?

Are they telling secrets?
Are they going to high-five?
Either way, it's fucking cute.

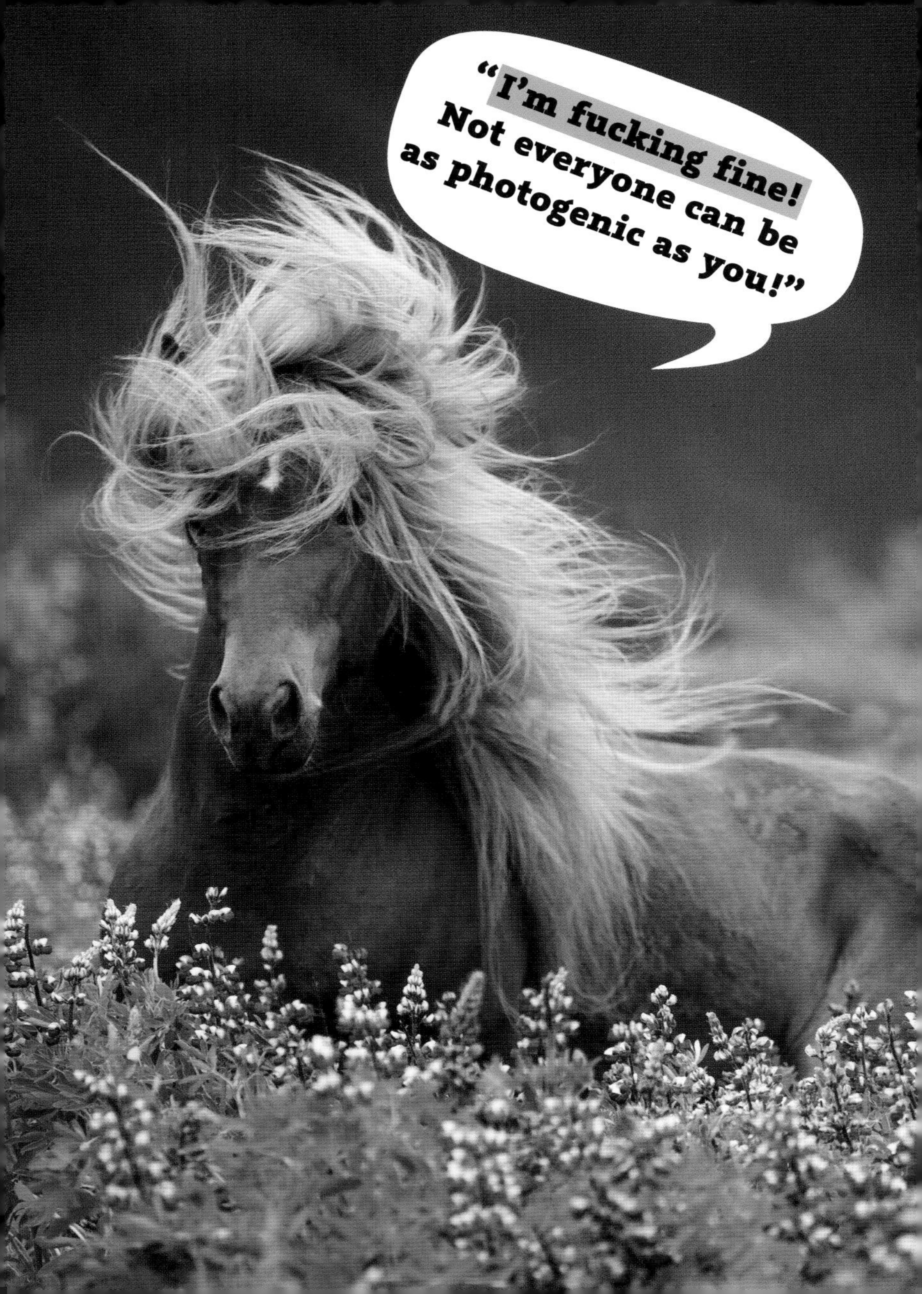
“I’m fucking fine! Not everyone can be as photogenic as you!”

The **utter fucking focus** on her face is damn perfect.

This is a fucking Christmas movie, you can't convince me otherwise!

Get that cute fucking face out of here!

She looks like she's **SWIMMING** in **FUCKING SUNSHINE!** What the fuck!

Of fucking **course** you're invited to the fucking **snuggle** party!

Fucking hell, a teddy bear? Will the cuteness never cease??

I **dare** any bitch to try not to smile at this **adorable shit**.

Why wasn't I invited to this **cute-as-fuck** family reunion?!

All these adorable family cuddles are going to make me fucking cry.

Okay **seriously**, I'm fucking sick of these adorable **pet friends**!

This **cute-ass** frog is about to tell the best **knee-slapper.**

You're too fucking cute to be so damn pouty!

Get those adorable **fucking feathers** out of my face!

Cows are just big fucking puppies, okay?!

How **THE HELL** do you get your hair to look that **fucking** good?

Don't give me that look.
I will snuggle the shit out of you!

This **friend-shaped** motherfucker is my new favorite animal!

He's about to
participate in
the cutest damn
stand-off!

Those cheeks are
fucking ridiculous...
ridiculously
ADORABLE!!

You fluffy fuck, open your eyes
and see how cute you are!

Those little whiskers are **fucking adorable.** I hope you're proud of yourself!

"MooooOOOOoo—
shit I'm out of
breath—
OOOOoooo
OOOOooom!"

All right, you might be cute as hell, but you don't need to be an ass about it!

This kiwi bird is way fucking sweeter than kiwi fruit!

Oh fuck off, you've got the cutest fucking yawn and you know it!

Get the fuck out of here with your cute little family moment!

Future's so bright, this bitch needs shades.

Who doesn't love a fucking Arctic dance battle?

It's a cute-ass elephant and it's running and it's too much to fucking handle!

If I see **ONE MORE** adorable tongue sticking out, I'm going to lose my shit!

I will *owlways* fucking love animals giving each other a peck!

Well, shit. These two goslings have danced their way **right** into my heart!

I **THINK** I passed out from the **adorableness** of these **damn rhinos!**

HOLY SHIT,
he fell for fall!

Do they look like a
cheesy movie poster?
Yes.
Am I obsessed with it?
Hell yes.

A unicorn, a ballerina, a bulldog — you can't just be all of the cute things!

The cutest siblings to ever exist? You better fucking believe it!

It's official:
this is the cutest
animal I've **ever seen**
in my **fucking life.**

WANT EVEN FUCKING *MORE* ADORABLE ANIMALS?

Spend your year looking at ridiculously fucking cute animals!

All the damn dogs you could possibly want, literally all year. Seriously, they're too fucking much.

Twelve whole months of the most adorable fucking cats you've ever seen!